HOW TO CHAT-UP MEN

Kitty Malone & Bunny Sylvester

SUMMERSDALE

Summersdale Publishers Ltd
46 West Street
Chichester
West Sussex
PO19 1RP
United Kingdom

Printed and bound in Great Britain.

ISBN 1 84024 050 4

Contents

HOW TO CHAT-UP MEN

8 How To Chat-up Men

One evening, a happy couple is driving home after dinner. A thought occurs to the woman, and without really thinking, she says it aloud, 'Do you realise that, as of tonight, we have been seeing each other for six months?'

And there is a silence in the car. To the woman, it seems like a very loud and long silence. And she thinks to herself, 'I wonder if he is feeling confined by our relationship; maybe he thinks I expect more commitment; maybe he was just about to tell me that he wanted to finish it. But, hey, maybe I'm not sure about all of this either. I mean, he's really nice but where is this relationship going?'

And the man is thinking, 'Gosh. Six months. So, that means it was . . . June when we met, and, hey, that's when I had to take the car into the garage, and this gearbox just still doesn't feel right.'

Men and women are different. Therefore, in order to win him, you must first try to understand him. For a man, his emotions are like taps on a bath . . . they can turn them off and on with no problems and the hotter and steamier the better. For a woman, her emotions are like a rollercoaster ride – it starts slowly, then gathers pace with lots of highs and lows, heaps of excitement before coming down to earth with a big bump.

Why risk chatting up a man? Simple, women know what they want and understand why they want it. (Men are unfortunately blinkered by a preoccupation with sex.) So she must learn to attract the various possibilities and then she can make her choice. Just as in the jungle, the female chooses.

Men do not understand women.

Man's (Limited) Thoughts on Woman

- She lives off yoghurt, cottage cheese, celery sticks and chocolate.
- She has two drinks and bursts into tears for no apparent reason.
- She spends days deciding what to wear before settling for the first outfit.
- She meets a man and, after a while, sleeps with him and immediately thinks this is 'the one.'
- She always says, 'What are you thinking about?' when he isn't thinking of anything.
- She is irrational, unreasonable, illogical and jealous.
- She gets even more irrational, unreasonable, illogical and jealous every 28 days.

This is, as we know, a very narrow view on the fairer sex. Women are much more open-minded . . .

Woman's (Limited) Thoughts on Man

'I want a man who is kind and understanding. Is that too much to ask of a millionaire?' – Zsa Zsa Gabor

We might as well lay the cards down on the table right at the beginning. What we would like is a solvent, single, charming, witty and honest man. We are probably realistic enough to realise that the arrival of a knight in shining armour on his white charger only happens in Hollywood films (anyway, all that armour would be hell to get him out off).

Chatting up isn't all about an aggressive assertion of women's rights and girl power. It is a careful and subtle affair that gently sorts the big boys from the bad boys and the best from the bastards.

Settling for second best is not an option and that is why many girls today are prepared to put in the groundwork. The secret, of course, is letting the man think that things are going just the way he wants them to, while you, naturally, have everything beautifully planned out from beginning to end.

Follow our Six P's Rule (*Proper Planning and Preparation Prevents Poor Performance*) and we hope that chatting up will no longer be a risky business for you but a profitable one.

ON BEING SINGLE

So, we would *like* a man. It is very important first of all to recognise that you don't ever *need* a man. They are an added extra – like a lovely garnish on a beautiful dish. They compliment it and enhance it and bring out all its best qualities. Before you decide to chat up a man you must be perfectly happy as you are – single.

Good things about being single:

- You can hog the whole bed
- The toilet seat gets left down
- You don't have to keep your legs perpetually smooth and bronzed
- You can shop until you drop with no one complaining
- You can flirt and pull whenever and whomever you want

The addition of a man into your life will ruin all of the above – even if he is a perfect man. So think carefully about the consequences and then if you decide that he won't interrupt your well planned days and you can cope with waiting for that phone to ring, take a deep breath and begin the hunt.

THE HUNTRESS

We have the vote. We wear suits. We control our reproductive system. We have our own mortgages, bank accounts and personal pension plans. We are prime ministers, chief executives and merchant bankers. We can manage a full time job *and* a full time family. In short, we have considerable power.

The once fearsome roar of the male of the species is now much less scary and the girls now hunt just as well as the boys. We can fend for ourselves, but the natural instinct to find a mate is still strong. It's just that our expectations are so much higher. The territories once marked out have been shifted and this has caused an understandable panic in the packs of males, as they are a little uncertain as to what to do. No longer is it simply enough for them to look good, we want more and that's why we're prepared to go out and find it.

Girls can chat up men.

THE HUNTED

Gone are the days when men could impress us simply by rubbing two sticks together and providing us with the next piece of meat. Today much more is expected from them than mere prowess at the BBQ. They should flatter us, charm us, understand us, converse cleverly with us, wine and dine us, trust us and love us. Unfortunately, it would seem that few have moved past the ogle-slobber-rub crotch-ogle-pass out ritual.

Men have always been on top for hundreds of years and now it is time for them to experiment with a few new positions. Understandably, they're not very good at it. But with a helping hand (or two) and a few nudges in the right direction they can perform well.

It is the men who face the biggest problems in the future as they have to adjust to their new and complicated roles. That is why it is important not to terrify them into submission and to reassure them that today's confident and intelligent woman appreciates a confident and intelligent man.

Men need to be chatted up.

ABOUT MEN

All women know that we are much better at understanding men than men are at understanding us, or relationships, or love, or emotions, or period pains. We know that men are preoccupied with sex and their manhood. We know that we must not flirt outrageously with other men, but it is perfectly acceptable for them to flirt with our girlfriends. Men ogle because they need to look around and reassure themselves that their woman is the most beautiful. We know what a man's perfect night would be . . .

Man's Perfect Night

1. Return home after successful day at work to beautiful girlfriend, partner, lover.
2. Fondle her breasts.
3. Catch up on the stock market and the sports results.
4. Have a beer and play computer games.
5. Go out with the lads for a curry and pints.
6. Attempt seductive moves in tacky nightclub.
7. Have a kebab and chips on the way home.
8. Attempt seductive moves in the bedroom.
9. Slobber over girl and proclaim eternal love.
10. Collapse into bed.
11. Wake, make love and find she has made a fresh coffee, ironed his shirts and found a supply of painkillers.

Men are simple creatures and easily pleased. They are most easily pleased by a quick snog and some rumpy-pumpy. Darwin's survival of the fittest theory dictates that men must spread their genes around as often as possible and they rely on women to spread their legs to help them. However, men do not necessarily respect the ones who readily oblige and, hypocritically, do not like the idea of a potential girlfriend sleeping around. But men are not all Casanovas. They just like to think that they are.

THE SELECTION

All men do have a little element of a Mr Casanova in them. They are an assorted group and infinitely diverse and that is part of the fun and part of their appeal. Here are just a few of them . . .

The footballer

He will be easily spotted by his naff hairstyle such as wet look perms or vividly dyed crops. He will often have a childhood sweetheart in tow, but may dribble with a Page 3 stunner from Swindon. Catch him early on in his career down at the local football club and that way you get the pick of the team. Weekends and evenings are generally devoted to the game although he might appreciate you watching from the sidelines and praising his skills afterwards. The fairy tale of Posh and Beckham is as about as likely as England winning the next World Cup.

Smooth army officer

He will be found at various military establishments around the country. He will have manners, he will be charming and he will look devastatingly handsome in his uniform. In 'civvies' he is another who favours red jeans and polo shirts. He will be extremely fit and the Cavalry officers have particularly strong thigh muscles. He will fight for Queen and country and he will fight for you too. The army officer may be the closest you are going to get to a knight in shining armour. However, they have a tendency to disappear to foreign wars, just as you have perfected how to polish their boots. He likes good girls to take home to Mummy and naughty girls for when he's on leave.

Surfer boy

He will be found at the beach and probably extremely fit, tanned and generally gorgeous. Unfortunately, he tends to be incredibly stupid with a limited vocabulary of mostly unintelligible words. You will have to be prepared to put up with endless hours spent on cold, windswept beaches watching a speck somewhere out on the waves (bad). He will like long, hot baths to ease the aching muscles and may well have a supply of other fit surfer mates to keep you amused (good). He likes sporty girls with sand between their toes and sun-bleached hair.

The teacher

He will either be the faded corduroys and the tweed jacket type or black Levi's and a second hand shirt variety. One is a musty, old headmaster who smells of pipe smoke and sherry. One is a smouldering, hip, vegetarian English tutor. His 9am classes are packed, as the girls are all happy to get out of bed for him. He'll take his pupils out after college but would never risk his reputation. He'll quote from the classics and educate your mind. He wants a girl with a passion for books, so read him like one and he might be great between the covers.

Pinstriped City trader

He will be found at city bars and in cheap London nightclubs (the ones with phones on the tables). He will be wearing a very expensive suit and designer shirt. Conversations will be monosyllabic and he will frequently glance at his pager for the latest update on the stock market. He keeps unsociable hours – very early mornings (to trade with Australia) and very late nights to meet with his clients (the bunny girls at Stringfellows). He's loaded and will spoil you rotten, but be careful – he's probably spoiling several others as well.

Mr Nice

This one will be the perfect gentleman, but good as this might sound, beware. There is something worrying about a man who is too nice. He will dress sensibly, nothing too outrageous, he'll be clean shaven and will live in a spotless house. He will take you out to lunch every week and pay every time, but remember that there's no such thing as a free lunch. It's up to you to find it out and soon. You'll probably be introduced through mutual friends who are always trying to fix him up with someone, but watch out. He has a secret lurking somewhere – strange habits, a long-term girlfriend or maybe he's even a closet gay.

Wannabe popstar

He prides himself on his salon-slicked hair, his designer shirts and his sunbed-acquired tan. He hangs out in trendy nightclubs and in expensive shops. Unfortunately, he hasn't quite made it and he will live in a bedsit with some other would-be stars all looking for that elusive break. He will tell you about his triumph at the local Karoke bar and promise that the EMI offer is arriving any day now. He'll be Jason for your Kylie and you can make sweet music together.

The Older Man

He will dress smartly and wear Italian loafers. He will run his own company that may or may not be successful. He will be found in the not-quite-but-almost trendy city clubs and try to impress the young traders with his knowledge of stocks and shares. He'll seem head-over-heels in love with you but his meek blonde wife will be waiting at home, as he has yet another late night meeting. He will definitely wine and dine you but he'll expect you for his pudding.

The Garage Mechanic

He will wear grimy overalls that will reveal a rippling chest (hopefully). He will cast loving eyes over your bodywork and admire all those curves. He's fantastic with his hands and knows what all the buttons are for. Find him fiddling round the back on the Porsche, the Jag or the MG. You can certainly expect a good servicing from him. And he'll look after your car pretty well too.

The Husband

Preferably he should be yours. He will be wearing a wedding ring, although the deceiving ones are sly enough to remove it. He will either be adoring and attentive (to his wife), or a charmer and a cheater (to his wife). To mess around with someone else's is not a very good idea. Remember that you will be exchanging the attentions of many men for the inattention of just one.

Men are not necessarily particularly choosy. If it looks like a woman (pad up those size AA's) then they'll be interested. Sometimes men have thoroughly bizarre tastes. Some men love the idea of a married woman, as Julie Birchill points out, *"Being married is incredibly attractive to the opposite sex and ensures that you will never go short of proposals."* Some men also like the idea of girls snogging each other. Not full on lesbian action, but a sort of extension of a girl's friendship for one another.

What we learn from this, is that men are peculiar creatures and want what they can't have, and specifically want what others do have. But they also like what no man has had. So you need to be a married lesbian who is a virgin with a wide sexual repartee.

What this means, girls, is that you need to be flexible, adjust to your particular man's current fantasy – go along with his ideas. If he really is the one, then, sooner or later, the *real* you will shine through, and if he isn't, well, it was always going to be hard to explain what an Austrian schoolgirl was doing holding down a job in the city and living somewhere in Shepherd's Bush.

So, that's men in a nutshell. What you must do is choose very carefully because at the end of the day it's *you* who makes the choice. Target many, but select one. Whatever his profession, deep down they tick the same way. Men think about sex almost all of the time. They think about relationships less of the time. The rest of it is divided between their mates, food and some form of social relaxation (which doesn't include you). However, before you make the selection, there is some planning and preparation to be done.

THE SIX P'S RULE

Proper Planning and Preparation Prevents Poor Performance

It's a jungle out there. Predators lurk and victims hide. Out comes your finest plumage and on goes your camouflage. Out comes your machete (for getting rid of the undergrowth) and on with your feelers (for discovering the fittest of the species). What you need is a few basic tips if you're going to survive: the first is that you must look and feel your best.

Plumage

Whilst some men may think that peephole bras and rubber body suits are the epitome of sexy dressing, there is *nothing* sexy about spending an evening wiggling on your chair to try and dislodge a wedgie caused by unfeasibly impractical underwear. An inch of mottled thigh being revealed by hold ups that have finally given in to the inevitability of gravity, unless you have the upper thighs of a supermodel, is also not seductive.

Before you go out, divide your clothes into two piles – those of *Past Pulling Power* and *Possible Pulling Potential*. Wear what you know you look good in and you will naturally feel comfortable and confident. Do try and leave something to the imagination – be a tease and offer a taster.

What you must *not* do is succumb to the temptation to go out and buy something special for that big night out. Especially avoid doing this with PMT; you may be convinced that you're going to be at your most irresistible wearing that turquoise mohair crop top, but you're not.

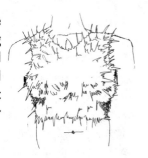

Unfortunately, it is Sod's law that when you do meet the man of your dreams, you will be wearing your old Mickey Mouse underwear that should have been chucked out when you left school, you won't have shaved your armpits for two weeks and your hair will be a greasy, tangled mess. But look on the bright side, you can only improve in his eyes.

Universally accepted sexy clothing

If your preference is for yellow polka dot bikinis then wonderful, but the following may just get him going . . .

• Boots

However, please, no moon boots, pixie boots, anything with a collar bit that makes your thighs look double the width they really are. Boots should preferably be knee length and well fitted.

• Underwear

To be worn under you clothing, unless you are going to a fancy dress party, or a fetish club or you wish to be unfavourably compared to Madonna. What is underneath though is important, because someone might just see it, and it shouldn't really be your grey M&S hip huggers.

• Stockings

Men just love the thought of that gap of the top of your legs and all those fastenings they can play with. Your legs must be smooth and, unfortunately, stockings are really only for the thin girls. Stockings have the disadvantage of having hooks at the back that requires you to dislocate your shoulder in order to do them up.

•*Rubber*

If you're into your watersports then a wet suit might just do it for that lifeguard. Rubber is absolutely fine if you have two people to help you in and out of it (might be right up your street). But, be warned, you will have to buy up Boots' talcum powder supply, and if you are going anywhere that involves a slight rise in temperature, you will soon start smelling like an abattoir. Also not suitable for anyone carrying surplus fat.

•*Leather*

Leather is just fab to the touch and suggests that you have that sex appeal necessary to lure your man. Try mail order from Anne Summers . . . but, like skin, leather has a tendency to leave stretch marks. Sitting for too long in leather trousers may leave general bagginess around the bum (this is not flattering).

• *Touchy-Feely Clothes*

Anything that will give him an excuse to stroke you is sexy – wear chenille, silk and velvet. Try to avoid anything nylon, as it will give him a nasty static shock when he rubs up too close to you (an advantage if you don't like him much).

•*Camouflage*

No advice here, as hopefully, you know best and if, orange eyeshadow and dark purple lipstick usually attracts the men, then keep applying it. In general though, keep the scarlet talons, brilliant poppy lips and lashings of mascara effect for nights out at the Rocky Horror show. Pastels may be fashionable, one legged trousers the next big thing, but are you really going to pull looking like a cross between Barbara Cartland and a victim of Edward Scissorhands?

Accessories

To ensure fully successful chatting up there are a few things that all girls should carry with them at all times.

- **A Powder Compact**
Use the mirror to see the people behind you and the powder to prevent a shiny nose.
- **Address and Phone Book**
Essential for inserting all the new ones and remembering the old ones.
- **A Fully Charged Mobile Phone**
For ringing friends, taxis, takeaways and for receiving those all-important calls.

•*A Lighter*
Even if you don't smoke – so you can offer your fire to handsome men.

•*A Scarf*
For tying up your hair, for being tied up with and for making your outfit look different the next day.

•*Sunglasses*
Think Jackie O, think sunshine, think ex-boyfriend in the same bar, think the morning after . . .

•*Condoms*
Just in case!

First of all, before we do any chatting up, we need to know where we are going to find all these single men waiting for a little of our encouragement.

The Hunting Grounds

The Pub

Avoid smoke-filled, old man pubs (unless you are specifically attracted to the dirty old man). Pubs are perfect, especially on a Friday night. The men and the women will all be up for it (you might have some competition), but pubs provide an excellent opportunity for circling and scanning the room before selecting a couple of targets.

Bars

A bit more sophisticated than the pub and you'll be likely to find your fair share of wide boys, salesmen and media types. Best of all, the barman could be a blonde, tanned Australian and you can ask

him for A Slow Comfortable Screw followed by a
Screaming Orgasm . . . without blushing.

Train

There is an enormous variety of possible pulls and you're also forced to sit side by side. This has advantages (you fancy the bloke next to you) and disadvantages (he is suffering from very bad breath). Unfortunately, people don't tend to talk much on trains but if you're really clever (and really forward) you could slip a piece of paper with his number on it into his pocket.

Sporting Events

The races, the dogs, football, rugby . . . the high emotional state of a crowd is an experience that you should make the most of. The warm glow of sharing a victory en masse may get the man next to you moving onto plenty of physical contact very early on. Equally, finding consolation in the arms of a fellow supporter can be a very successful strategy.

Weddings

Emotions are running high and everyone's thinking about love. Beware, however, of frightening off a potential pull by gazing too wistfully at the bride and groom. Instead, some sensible words about the admiration you have for the happy couple's brave decision may relax him. Try and be the bridesmaid.

Housewarmings

The key to success on this occasion is that excessive consumption of alcohol occurs when everyone is asked to bring a couple of bottles and it's then all mixed up in the bath. Everyone will be full of good spirits – alcoholic and otherwise.

The Gym

Fit, toned bodies (and that's just yours), clad in Lycra. An excellent opportunity to look at the goods before you purchase, as a muscle isn't the only thing you might pull at the gym. Just be aware that the men found in the gym may be more interested in their own, and each other's bodies, rather than yours.

Hospitals

The doctor/patient relationship is best avoided. Doctors also do not have much time and will be called away to help other girls in distress. Fake a sprained ankle and go in and have a look around. The shared experience of concern and pain can be a bonding one, but avoid those men visiting the maternity wards.

Something else for consideration is whether you go about this alone or in packs. Alone is hard if you are somewhere full of groups (such as pubs and clubs). Generally, we think that you need your girlfriends for encouragement, laughter and comforting you if he's not being susceptible to your charms. Being part of a large group can be difficult and, if you've decided tonight-is-the-night, then two of you should be plenty. It has to be a good friend though and perhaps an already attached one is useful, as then there's no one to compete with!

GETTING ON WITH IT

So, just how do you chat up a man? Each girl has her own ways, means and methods. What we believe is that there are certain things that every girl can do which will lure your man of choice over to you, and then it's over to him to do a bit of work. You attract, you flirt, you charm and you decide. It's all about sending out the right signals.

Body Language – Part I – Flirtation

Whether standing or sitting there are several ways to indicate your interest from fifty feet away. Masses of eye contact is the really obvious one and it should become clear that sooner or later you can move from fluttering eyelashes to a fluttering heart.

The Look
The way you look at a man will have a profound effect on him. Giggly sideways glances in conjunction with much whispering with girlfriends will draw his attention to you, and his curiosity and desire to have his ego caressed may well prove successful.

Spanner eyes tighten his nuts. A direct, lusting look will often be enough to drag a man, drawn by an indefinable magnetic attraction, away from the side of a leggy blonde to dance attendance at your side. Just keep staring at him and he will eventually succumb.

Do's and Don'ts of Body Language

Do Not:

- Collapse in a chair, in a short skirt which reveals your thighs
- Stand with your legs more than shoulder width apart and your hands on your hips – it is not a powerful come-and-get-me-then poise, it isn't attractive and you'll probably terrify him.
- Sit with your arms folded and your legs crossed – this is the opposite of the come-and-get-me position. It smacks of lack of confidence and uncertainty.
- Keep pulling at the hem of your short skirt, as although this will draw attention to your legs and bum, it will only make you look uncomfortable.

Do:

- Point your body in his direction (not thrusting hips and tits, but your general position should be facing him).
- Smile lots (but check that you've flossed your teeth beforehand).
- Sit or stand up straight (this has the general advantage of not making you look like an extra from the Hunchback of Notre Dame and will appear to add 3 inches to both your height and bra size).
- Cross your legs elegantly when sitting down and, if you are comfortable in heels, then wear them. As Marlene Dietrich said, '*The legs aren't so beautiful, I just know what to do with them.*

- Look confident. Tricky one to explain, but the above will all help and if you are with friends then you should be feeling relaxed anyway. (Remember that too much alcohol does not improve your confidence especially when you turn pale green and vomit at his feet.)

Top Flirty Things To Do (Drawing Attention To The Sexy Parts Of Your Body)

- Lean down and stroke your ankle (this has the added benefit of revealing your cleavage).
- Twiddle with the wispy bits of your hair behind your ear (no violent hair flicking from side to side).
- Speak softly to him so that he is forced to lean closer towards you. Also use light physical contact – don't be all over him like a rash, but just a gentle touch to his forearm every now and then will give him goosebumps.
- Play with your mouth and lick your lips in a suggestive manner. No slobbering.
- Stand near to him, as men will be more reluctant to approach you if you are sitting with a group of girls (intimidating).

Body Language – Part II – The Whole Package

Most of all, it is important to be yourself. However, there's no harm in having a bit of fun and bringing out your more playful side every now and again. Also, if things start going horribly wrong, then at least you've got your not-quite-true personality to hide behind. Judge your man wisely, and ask yourself what he really, really wants.

Aggressive and Assertive
Develop a strong bar presence, send him over a drink, walk over and inform him that you will be leaving together in 5 minutes.

Outrageously sexy

Look straight at him, arms gently on the hips (nothing too strident though), tits forward, legs crossed and knees pointing straight at him (if you are sitting down). Flick your hair occasionally and blatantly rest your hands near your most sensitive erogenous areas. He will instantly know that you are a complete sexual animal.

Sweet and Compliant

Avoid direct eye contact, unless you have your chin down and are looking at him through long lashes. Be interested, no, live for, his story of the football changing room incident, laugh at his jokes, flatter his ego. Be innocent, sensitive and virginal and mix it with a very short skirt for a heady combination.

Downright feisty

Perhaps a modified combination of 'aggressive' and 'outrageously sexy'. Be charmingly reluctant to give him any personal information, like your phone number, and play the hard-to-get card. Slightly undermine his ego, suggest that you think he is not quite as attractive as he thinks he is, but he'll do and send him the signal that you are still quite interested to see what is in his lunch box. The independent, successful, attractive woman who takes no shit is a steamy combination for a man who is looking for fun without too much responsibility. Make him realise that might be just what you are looking for too. Hard to pull off well, but the not-too-forward-but-ever-so-sure-of-herself approach usually works a treat.

Bimbo

He thinks this is going to be the quickest and easiest pull of his life. Blondes know how quickly men will jump to certain assumptions. Use this to your advantage, girls – catch him off guard and show him what you are really made of. Stun him with your looks and your knowledge of his car's mechanical workings and he will find the visual and intellectual dichotomy an endless source of fascination.

Innocent Abroad

This one is a real favourite. Men love foreign girls, mainly because women on holiday seem to loose their sexual scruples. They think this is an ideal opportunity for some ridiculously casual sex, and being territorial creatures, they like to think that they are giving one to the whole of the European sub-continent, and someone who might be distantly related to Ulrika Jonsson. Be warned that it will be hard work keeping up a Swedish or American accent for any length of time, and harder still when you are sober.

Body Language – Part III – Drastic Measures

Here you could play the damsel-in-distress card, but, be careful, as men aren't very good with emotional things and may just be very scared and turn to your more-in-control-of-herself mate.

Fainting, crying, trembling, looking distraught and faking an asthma attack (it has been known) all present you with opportunities to collapse into his arms.

Basically, men aren't really going to mind what you say or do, if *you* are confident enough to give *them* the confidence to make more of a move than a lecherous one.

You know things are working when . . .

- He's talking to you and paying attention, even if his mates are there.
- He's drooling.
- He's buying you drinks (keep an eye on how many).
- He's making a lot of physical contact (stroking your arm, brushing against you).
- He asks for your number.
- He asks if you have a boyfriend.

GETTING DOWN TO IT

So, you've lured him, caught him and made him want you. If your chatting up has been successful and you have decided that he has potential, then you will want to see him again. Hopefully, he will be so utterly captivated and taken with you that he will ask for your number and camp out on your front doorstep.

Things become more tricky when he isn't forthcoming with his right lines, or it's that awkward 'morning after' situation. Remember that the initial stages of courtship are always fraught with dangers and you must decide whether he seems genuine (often virtually impossible to tell), or if all he's after is a one-night stand. We dream of a man going to the trouble of remembering where you work, finding out the address and phoning you out of the blue. In reality, the only thing he can probably remember is his name.

How To Give Him Your Number (Without Him Realising)

- Write it down with a 'Well, then?' and slip it into his jacket pocket.
- Scribble it on a beer mat and throw it at him (this requires accuracy) or place in front of him.
- Give it to a friend of his and hope they will work out your scheme (dangerous as a girl might be jealous and rip it up, and a bloke might think it's for him).
- Scrawl it somewhere on his shirt or skin (only possible when he is very drunk).
- Follow him home in a taxi and push it through his letter box (a bit desperate).
- Go home with him in a taxi and leave it behind on his pillow (very friendly).

The Direct Approach

Don't be too 'keen' and give away your number to every man who has a passing fancy to your backside. It should be a very select few. There may be occasions on which the man is simply too good to let go of. Summon up your courage, unclasp his hand and look steadily into his eyes. You must be strong enough to cope with the fact that the following approaches do not come with a satisfaction guarantee.

If you really want something these days then you have to go and get it. (No girl should risk humiliation though, so do target carefully.)

Approach I – Asking For It

'So, may I have your number then?'
This is to be said with a coy sideways glance and huge amounts of flirtation.

Approach II – Giving It To Him

'You're quite simply the most gorgeous man in the room and I can't leave without giving you my number.'
This one will flatter his ego. Use the same delivery style as above.

Approach III – Seeking Him Out

Men are creatures of habit often returning to the same watering holes and hunting grounds; they like an environment that they have scented well, the urinals of their local, for example. It is often possible to 'casually bump' into to your target, by using a little lateral planning as to their potential whereabouts.

Approach IV – Simplicity

This can often be staggeringly successful. When he walks past, or if you are now alongside, simply give him a sideways glance, whisper 'hello' coyly and walk seductively over to a friend nearby. He will want to know more.

Approach V – The Food Of Love

They say that the way to a man's heart is through his stomach. Tell him that you have just finished a Cordon Bleu cookery course and would he like to taste what you're offering? Invite him round for supper and if you can actually cook, all the better. If not then book a restaurant, and when he arrives at your place, say that you thought going out would be more fun.

We should also deal with the poor unfortunates, who have been entranced by your flirtations and are now glued to your skirt every time you turn around. They must be quickly got rid of, before all the other men in the room think that you are a taken woman. So, how do you avoid him if you discovered you have made a horrible error of judgement? Having eyed him up across the bar, on finally speaking to him, you discover that, due to the fact that his testicles never dropped, he has a speaking voice like Aled Jones on speed, Bugs Bunny teeth and breath like a medium ripe Camembert.

You will now have to embark on advanced chatting up, which, hypocritically, involves backtracking rapidly and not doing any chatting up at all.

The Method

Hold your glass firmly in front of you, moving it to parry any potential invasion of your personal space. Suddenly grab your stomach, just to the bottom left of your tummy button, and exclaim, 'Woah, ovulating again! Those little buggers just keep popping out!' – men hate anything gynaecological. If all else fails, just grab the nearest tall, handsome and well-built man standing around at the bar and say to your pursuer, 'Do meet my fiancee, he is a Tae Kwon Do black belt, you know.' With any luck, you bemused knight in shining armour may well become your next hot water bottle.

COURTSHIP – EARLY STAGES

Congratulations – he has got your number and/or you have got his. So, who calls? Do you put yourself out of your misery and pick up the phone or do you spend all afternoon staring at the life-line to the outside world?

A difficult one this, but generally if you want to avoid hurt and rejection, then it's going to have to be up to him. But, if he doesn't call, and you played it casual, then on no account go through the phone book using a process of elimination and whittling it down to a list of fifty possible Smiths living in the local telephone directory (it has been done).

From recent polls done in our offices, men think it is acceptable to leave it 6-9 days to call, women think the man should call in 3-4. Bear this in mind before you ring the bastard up on day 5 in tears.

Of course, whilst it would be ideal if he called you up the next morning, you are allowed to ask him out (gulp). Keep it casual, maybe with a few friends, and strictly during daylight hours. But, don't move too fast, men operate at two speeds, the one they think at and the one they drive at.

Money

Rule number one: if you aren't quite sure if you like him, he pays – every time. Rule number two: if you've decided that you *do* like him, he pays. But seriously, if you are chatting him up regularly over the food of love, then at least offer to pay your way, as there's no need to go so far as to pay for him as well. Then it looks less like he has to pay for your company and you will feel less like a high-class prostitute. A woman should have her financial independence regardless of whether she's buying fish and chips or caviar.

E-mail

If you have it, use it. We like e-mail. You can add his address to your address book (phone up his work place and ask for their company e-mail). Then you can forward a joke to everyone and if this little offering is no spur to his conscience, then you can assume that it's going no further. You can send something a few times just to make sure. The beauty of e-mail is that you can tell exactly when he got it and somehow deathly silence in cyberspace seems less hurtful. Besides, you can always blame a power surge for the failure of any response to your witty message.

Intimacy

We are not offering any advice about how quickly your courtship should progress. The decision to sleep with a man is above all, *your* choice – never do it because you think this will guarantee the man's commitment. You may be a complete sex goddess, but the man will only truly stay with you if you can offer him a bit more than fantastic frolics every night. Trust us.

COURTSHIP – ADVANCED STAGES

Now you have your man, what do you do with him? The adjustment from singledom to coupledom need not be an extreme jump and often as little change in his life as possible will keep him very happy. There is always an element of comfort in a relationship but it should never become a routine.

Keeping it up

- Go away for the weekend to a seedy hotel in a coastal location where there'll be sun, sea, sand and . . .
- Surprise him – anything from turning up with no underwear on to giving him a spontaneous massage.
- Take the day off work and go somewhere different together.
- Send him a card or a letter and list all the reasons why you like him.
- Go back to the place where you first met, or the first restaurant you went to together, and chat him up all over again.
- Take charge for the evening – tell him where and when you want him, ply him with food and drink, and offer yourself for pudding.
- If you're out with a group of friends, then whisper romantic or dirty thoughts in his ear.

COURTSHIP – BAD STAGES

Is he the man of your dreams? If it's more the stuff of nightmares then sooner or later niggling doubts will inevitably start to surface. It often starts though when couples forget that chatting up should continue in a relationship. All of us have been guilty of indulging in bad habits if things aren't quite going well . . .

Women's Bad Habits

- Blatantly chatting up other men in front of your man – you did it once so why undo all your good work?
- Talking lots about ex's
- Not making an effort – legs and armpits should really be kept hair free and try to keep your underwear matching. You should want him to always fancy you, otherwise his attention may wander.
- Taking cigarettes without asking and expecting him to buy all of the drinks.
- Telling him that you want more space or that you think you should just be friends.
- Putting pressure on him to buy that diamond ring after the second date.

Men's Bad Habits

- No longer caring if bodily functions (such as belching and farting) are performed in front of you, and even worse, in front of other people.
- Leaving piles of dirty clothes at your house and expecting a store of ironed shirts.
- Not shaving for days because he thinks you might like the stubble look. We don't. It hurts.
- Groping you in an extremely jealous manner when they are drunk, especially in public.
- Telling all their mates about your sexual exploits.

The problem with bad habits is that they will *really* start to annoy after a while. Unfortunately, this is a classic danger sign of a doomed relationship. Some of the above habits you might find endearing in your man and maybe you quite like the sexy stubble look, but, generally, once they start to annoy, believe us, it gets worse.

Please don't be an ostrich and stick your hand in the sand. Have the courage to realise that you've made a mistake.

Terminal danger signs (for men and women)

- Breakdown in communication – no flirty emails, no little love notes, no late night phone calls, in fact you hardly know what he's up to.
- Spending lots of time with your friends and always making excuses as to why you don't want to see him.
- Repulsion vibes – you just physically can't stand to be near him and any contact makes you want to run a mile.
- Infidelity – we've all done it (it can be excused) but not on a regular basis.

Remember that when you find yourself with just the one man eating out of your hands then do not *ever* take him for granted. You have beguiled and captivated him, and he has decided that you are worth it. If you cheat on him, then expect revenge . . . men, just like women, certainly don't take kindly to unfaithfulness.

BREAKING UP

Sometimes though, despite your most effective chatting up and working away at keeping up a good relationship, the end result is obviously not going to be a marriage made in heaven. If you make a break, then make it a clean one. Treat him as you would want to be treated, and with any luck, you will have him right where you want him.

Accept, learn and move on. Also, be brave enough to recognise if the fruits of your labours are not making him happy, because, if that's the case then it won't be right for you either.

If you're feeling really miserable then you need some pick-me-ups. These are good for any occasion when life is a bit blue . . . after all, there will always be moments when the job is frustrating, when the mortgage payments stop you from buying that perfect suit and when the love life is either non-existent or would quite frankly be better if it was so.

Blues Beaters

- Put on your favourite CD and (if the house is empty) sing very loudly to it.
- Raid the drinks' cabinet and make yourself a chilled cocktail.
- Pamper yourself – a relaxing bubble bath followed by a manicure.
- Phone a girlfriend and talk about all the men who make you spine tingle.
- Curl up somewhere comfortable and read some of your favourite book.
- Write a letter to a friend who you have not been in touch with for a while.
- Arrange something to look forward to in the next few weeks.
- And anything else that you know makes *you* feel happy . . .

AND FINALLY . . .

Remember, chatting up is, above all, fun.
And if you don't quite get your man the first time
then the next one is always just around the corner.
Practise makes perfect . . .

CHAT-UP LINES . . .

Is that a gun in your pocket
or are you just pleased to see me?
(No, it's a gun.)

You remind me of my last holiday . . .
it wasn't long enough.

My name's Holly. I'll chat you up if you like
because I'm used to little pricks.

Would you like to look up my skirt?
(Yes!)
It's on page sixty-five of this catalogue.

I'm not wearing anything under this dress.
(Would you like me to recommend a clothes shop?)

What would you do if you ever
got chatted up by a woman?
(Warn her that I used to be one.)

How would you like my eggs in the morning?

I'm a bit busy this week, but I'd like to squeeze
in a date with you . . . trouble is I'm worried
that you might not be much of a squeeze.

Hello, you don't know me, but I've just come back from the future in which you and me have the most passionate love affair. And it started tonight, actually.

Hello, I'm from an underwear company.
We're conducting free spot-checks on men to
make sure their underwear is the right size for them.
Just breathe in when my hands are in place . . .

I'd like to have your baby.
(Go ahead and take it.)

Are you an undercover policeman,
or isn't that a truncheon?

Other Humour Books from Summersdale

Chat-up Lines and Put Downs
Stewart Ferris   £3.99

More Chat-up Lines and Put Downs
Stewart Ferris   £3.99

How To Chat-up Women (Pocket edition)
Stewart Ferris   £3.99

Enormous Boobs
The Greatest Mistakes In The History of the World
Stewart Ferris   £4.99

101 Uses for a Losing Lottery Ticket
Shovel/Nadler   £3.99

Men! Can't Live with them, Can't live *with* them
Tania Golightly   £3.99

Girl Power
Kitty Malone   £3.99

The Kama Sutra For One
O'Nan and P. Palm   £3.99

101 Reasons Not To Do Anything
*A Collection of Cynical
and Defeatist Quotations*   £3.99

A Little Bathroom Book £3.99

Available from all good bookshops.